Scientific Pioneers

Five Incredible Tales of People Who Helped Develop the Scientific Method

Nury Vittachi
Illustrations by Step Cheung

Contents

THE WOMAN WHO HID THE MOON

SOMETIMES YOU'D THINK IT would be tough to be a girl in the olden days. There was no such thing as "women's rights" and men were in charge of most things outside the home.

Yet we should not think that women were oppressed throughout history until modern times. Remember, human society itself evolves, and in the long run we arrange things to the best advantage of all members of humanity, female and male.

If we study history, we notice that in every era, there were many women who did amazing things, and were often leaders, from Boudica (say "Bow-di-ka") in the UK to the Chinese Empress Xiaozhuangwen (say "She-ow, ju-ang, wen").

Here's a really interesting example. Some time in the second century BC, a woman named Hegetor had a daughter named Aglaonike (pronounced "Agla-o" and then "Ni-ke", like the sports shoe).

Aglaonike loved the sky and spent hours watching the movements of the stars. During the daylight hours, she would study the writings of the great thinkers of the times.

She lived in Greece. In those days, in the centuries before the birth of Christ, her homeland produced a huge amount of the world's most important thinkers and greatest discoveries.

Aglaonike joined a group called The Witches of Thessaly, a group of clever women who were famous from the third century to the first century BC.

Now it may seem odd to have someone whose title was "witch" in a science book. But remember, for most of history, people were very open-minded, and all sorts of different forms of knowledge were blended together. And even today, open-mindedness is considered a key quality of a good scientist.

One day, Aglaonike realized something. From her sky charts, she knew that the moon would soon undergo an eclipse.

The moon would begin its period in the sky looking like it was full, a bright disk.

But then the shadow of the earth would fall over it — and it would disappear as if someone was taking bites out of it.

She decided to make a big announcement, to demonstrate the power of knowledge. On a certain night soon approaching, people could watch as a force would "take the moon down from the sky", she said.

Surely not!

How could such a thing happen?

Excitement spread and people gathered that night to watch. It was very dark: there were no lights of course, so they had candles and torches, or just sat under the starlight (no light pollution or smog in those days, lucky them).

And just as Aglaonike had said, the moon began to disappear.

Her name became part of a popular proverb in those days.

Say a person asked you to do something and you wanted to emphasize your agreement. Instead of just nodding and saying "yes", you would say: "Yes, as the moon obeys Aglaonike."

THE MAN WHO STAYED IN HIS HOUSE FOR TEN YEARS

A LITTLE OVER ONE THOUSAND years ago, a cross, hard-hearted prince named Al-Hakim was born in Egypt. He became Caliph (which means "leader") at the age of 11, in the year AD 996.

He was a tough person who had his critics put to death and churches destroyed.

People were scared of him and worried about what he was doing to society.

The Caliph's wise man was so upset that he felt he was losing his mind and told his staff to lock him away.

For the next 10 years, the Caliph continued to rule the land in a harsh way. When a barking dog kept him awake at night, he banished all dogs from the land. He did not like certain vegetables and shellfish, so he made them illegal.

Then one night, the Caliph went out at night on a donkey by himself, as was his habit, and never returned. The donkey and a blood-stained garment were found — so perhaps one of his citizens killed him.

The leaders of the community met to decide which of the princes should be the next leader.

But while this was taking place, something remarkable happened. Remember the Caliph's wise man, who had gone crazy?

He asked to talk to the nobles and explained that he had not really gone crazy at all. His name was Ibn Al-Haytham, and he explained that the Caliph had given him an impossible assignment. He knew that he would fail and the punishment would be that he would be put to death.

So he had pretended to be mad, so that he would be locked up instead.

Al-Haytham turned out to be a very interesting person. He had been a Cairo-born youth of just 19 years old when the Caliph had been born.

Al-Haytham's interest had always been astronomy, and when he heard that that the new young leader was also interested in science, he thought they would work together happily.

Al-Haytham had got a job as a wise man in the palace.

But the Caliph Al-Hakim had demanded that the young wise man oversee a project to turn the desert green.

Al-Haytham had studied the plans and realized that the project would fail — and failure always meant death.

So he had pretended to go mad.

What had Al-Haytham done for the 10 years he had spent in one house? "I did a lot of thinking, and experiments," he revealed. "And I wrote a book."

And what a book it was! Al-Haytham's work was called "The Book of Optics" and it was a masterpiece, seven volumes long. It was all about light.

Al-Haytham had spent a lot of his time looking out of the window of the house in which he had been imprisoned. He saw the bright noonday sun. He saw the interestingly hazy light of twilight. He saw the colors of dawn and sunset. He saw rainbows after the rain. He saw the strange silvery-blue brightness of moonlight, which seemed to remove colours from the things on which it shone.

He made observations and then wrote about how light

worked: how it travelled in straight lines but could be distorted by glass and water; how colors worked; how things are reflected in mirrors at certain angles; and how our eyes work.

Al-Haytham was very smart, and most of his findings were new, valuable pieces of information.

But this important Islamic scientist did much more than just tell the world about light. He was so careful with his experiments and observations that he taught us about the importance of making hypotheses and testing them before deciding they were facts which could be trusted. He was one of the originators of what is now called the scientific method.

The history of science includes contributions from all the main cultures of the world, and Muslim scientist Al-Haytham is one who will always be remembered — even if he spent a big portion of his life as a crazy locked-up lunatic.

THE BOY WHO WAS CURIOUS ALL HIS LIFE

OH BOTHER! SHEN KUO was sick again. The little boy was always getting some illness or another. He was stuck at home, day after day, feeling bad.

His parents, minor government workers, were not rich, but could afford to hire doctors to give him health potions, and fengshui experts to make sure he was sleeping in the right place.

But despite not having riches or health, little Shen Kuo had something else that would change the world: he had an enormous sense of curiosity.

Why this? Why that? Why the other?

When doctors fed him foul medicines, he wanted to know what was in them and what they did. And when the fengshui master knew which way was south, the boy asked: "But how do you know?"

Curiosity can be a good thing for a student to have, and when Shen Kuo recovered, he did very well in his exams. His community, in the seaside town of Xiamen on the coast of China in the AD 1040s, congratulated him.

When Shen Kuo reached his 20s, he no longer became ill regularly, but still had his sense of curiosity. When faced with a problem of dealing with swampland on assignment for the local government, he studied the problem and made a drainage system which turned it into the finest farmland.

He zoomed up the ladder and became famous as a polymath, which is a person who is brilliant at a wide range of things, from poetry to science.

One day, as an adult, he sat in his garden at his home and wrote a book called "Dream Pool Essays", about all the things he was curious about. It featured discoveries ranging from "How the Sun Makes Rainbows" to "How to Use a Mineral Called Orpiment to Rub Out Mistakes on Paper." He said there was such a thing called "Dragon Fire", a type of blaze which burned more brightly when you poured water on it. It sounds strange, but he was right — think of petrol fires, or chip-pan fires.

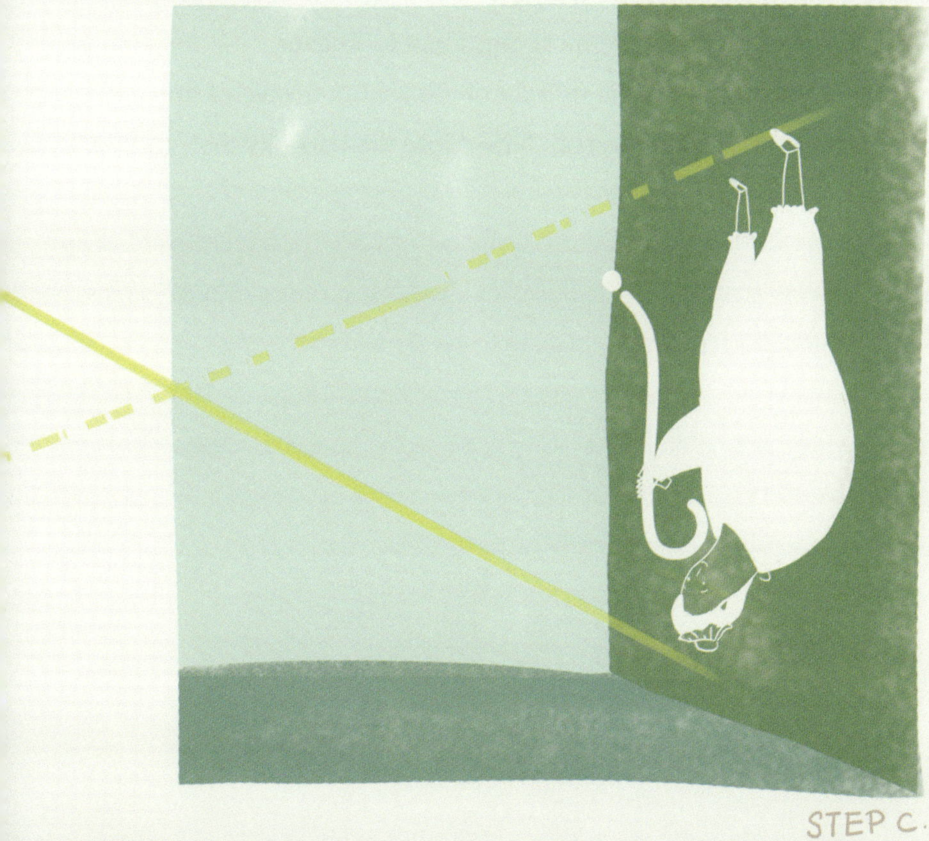

But he never forgot the things that made him curious when he was a child. So he wrote about how medicines worked.

And he also wrote the first known scientific description of how to make a compass, a secret that fengshui masters had known for centuries. Geomancers would rub the tip of a needle with a rock called a lodestone and dangle it from a single thread of silk tied halfway along it. Like magic, the needle would always find south. (Traditionally, Western compasses are made to point north, while Chinese ones are made to point south.)

By the year 1111, Chinese sailors were using compasses to find their way around the world, and they spread around the world to become one of the most important tools ever.

Shen Kuo's book taught us a lot of things. But it was his life that taught us the biggest lesson: Never lose the curiosity that you had as a child.

THE GRUMPY NUN WHO WAS FORBIDDEN TO SING

CHRISTIANS TRADITIONALLY GIVE 10 per cent of everything they get to the local church.

So when a Christian family had their 10th child, they decided to give the entire girl as a gift to the local monastery!

That might sound like an odd thing to do, but the girl herself was delighted. Her name was Hildegard of Bingen, and she was very spiritual.

Despite being only seven years old, she was keen to devote her life to the big questions of life.

In the year 1106 she arrived at an ancient monastery in Germany and started training to be a nun (think of Julie Andrews in the movie "The Sound of Music").

It suited her perfectly, and by the time Hildegard was an adult, she was the head of the women's section, with the title of Abbess.

But all her life, Hildegard had an independent streak.

One day, she decided that women should have a separate monastery, because men were so bossy.

So she announced that she was "very firm" about her decision to move to her own building, and pretended to have turned to stone. She just sat there. She refused to move a muscle until the head abbot said yes.

So she became chief of her own all-girl monastery, and there she wrote many books about science and music and religion and nature — all of which were a single subject in those days. This was in the 1100s, when few people were recording knowledge in books.

Even when Hildegard was an old woman in her 80s, she still had a naughty streak.

A man who had misbehaved died and she showed him forgiveness, agreeing to give him a burial space.

But this was against the rules. Local church bosses said they would dig him up again. But they couldn't because she refused to tell them where he was buried.

"I've hidden him," she laughed.

Furious, they excommunicated her whole monastery and made a rule forbidding her and the other women to ever sing again.

Now that was a sad, silent time for the women's monastery.

But Hildegard wrote to the church's top bosses, who thought she was a smart, good person, and forgiving the evildoer was the Christian thing to do. They overturned the verdict of the local chiefs.

Now she and "her girls" could sing once more.

After Hildegard died, people discovered that as well as the expected hymns and plays, she had written many books of knowledge — and she went down in history as an important early scientist. She wrote a lot about herbs and medicinal plants, and her work influenced the way that people think about natural elements as the best sort of medicine there is.

Today, there are more women than men in spiritual groups, and many people like to remember Hildegard, the tough, cheeky visionary who started life as a gift to the church, and ended it as a gift to humanity.

THE BOY WHO SORTED OUT THE LIVING WORLD

THREE HUNDRED YEARS AGO, there lived a poor church pastor called Linnaeus who had a little boy called Carl. The garden outside their house sloped down to a lake.

The churchman often combined his main sources of pleasure, by sitting with his son in the garden, teaching him about the different parts of a flower.

Little Carl was inspired, and by the age of eight, he could describe all 400 plants in his father's collection.

At first, the pastor was very proud of his son. But then the boy's enthusiasm for nature became a problem.

Carl had no interest in his school lessons — he just wanted to spend his time exploring the forests.

When the boy was 10, the pastor saved up enough money to send him to a school far away from the local woodlands of the place where they lived in Sweden.

But the boy soon found an interesting piece of woodland near the school, and preferred to spend his time there, instead of studying his books.

His parents were worried. They hoped that Carl would become a pastor and take over his father's job — but how could a man earn a living if he knew nothing but varieties of flowers?

Then a teacher at school realized that the fact that Carl preferred the forest to books might not be a bad thing. Perhaps he could become a botanist, which is an expert on plants.

By the time the boy was 17, Carl was reading strange, ancient "books of herbs" day and night.

And when he went to university, he devised a system of classification: a way of listing living things according to the shapes and functions of their parts.

Using his system, you could pick up any plant in the world and work out which family it belonged to, how it would reproduce itself and so on.

By the time he was an adult, he became interested in animals too, and worked out a way to classify them as well.

He did the job so well that the Linnaeus system came to be

STEP C

used by scientists all over the world to preserve their knowledge of the living world.

One of the things scientists do, following Carl Linnaeus' system, is to declare one example of each plant or animal as the Type Specimen and describe it in an official record.

If you look up the official science records for the Type Specimen for a species known as Homo sapiens (yes, that's you and me), you'll find a description of a certain Swedish man with fair hair and brown eyes.

Yes, the first scientifically classified human being was Carl Linnaeus himself!

KEEP READING

READING ABOUT THE LIVES of scientists and other discoverers adds to our store of knowledge, but we hope also leads us towards something much greater, which is wisdom.

This book is part of a series, which we hope you'll enjoy reading, and will spur you on to do your own scientific research.

The creators of this book wish you success in your explorations.

THE YOUNG SCIENTISTS SERIES

Book 1: SECRETS IN THE ROCKS
Five Astounding Tales of People Solving Mysteries Beneath Our Feet

Book 2: FABULOUS PHYSICS
Five Amazing Stories of People Who Solved Nature's Puzzles

Book 3: MAGICAL MATHEMATICS
Five Astonishing Stories of People Who Did Miracles with Numbers

Book 4: BREAKERS OF BARRIERS
Five Stunning Stories of People Demolishing Walls to Make History

Book 5: SCIENTIFIC PIONEERS
Five Incredible Tales of People Who Helped Develop the Scientific Method

Book 6: THE AMAZING QUANTUM
Five Awesome Stories of People Who Made a Revolution in Physics

Book 7: THE SCIENCE OF HUMANITY
Five Fascinating Stories of People Who Helped Us Understand Ourselves

Book 8: WOMEN OF DISCOVERY
Five Super Stories of Fabulous Females Who Made Scientific History

Book 9: THE INVENTOR'S SPARK
Five Marvelous Stories of People Who Helped Shape the Modern World

Book 10: ADVANCES IN ALCHEMY
Five Startling Stories of Chemistry and Biology

Book 11: THE CALL OF THE STARS
Five Wonderful Stories of People Looking to the Heavens

Book 12: MYSTERIES OF NATURE'S LAWS
Five Striking Stories of People Investigating the Deepest Puzzles of Reality

Published by

WS Education, an imprint of
World Scientific Publishing Co. Pte. Ltd.
5 Toh Tuck Link, Singapore 596224
USA office: 27 Warren Street, Suite 401-402, Hackensack, NJ 07601
UK office: 57 Shelton Street, Covent Garden, London WC2H 9HE

National Library Board, Singapore Cataloguing in Publication Data
Name(s): Vittachi, Nury, 1958– | Cheung, Step, illustrator.
Title: Scientific pioneers : five incredible tales of people who helped develop the scientific method / author, Nury Vittachi ; illustrator, Step Cheung.
Other title(s): Young scientists series ; 5.
Description: Singapore : World Scientific Publishing Co Pte Ltd, 2017.
Identifier(s): OCN 969703376 | ISBN 978-981-3221-48-2 (paperback)
Subject(s): LCSH: Scientists--Juvenile literature. | Science--Juvenile literature.
Classification: DDC 509.22--dc23

British Library Cataloguing-in-Publication Data
A catalogue record for this book is available from the British Library.

All royalties received will be channelled to the National Book Development Council of Singapore (NBDCS) as a gift from the author.

First published 2017
Reprinted 2018

Printed in Singapore